For a better life
Fearlessness

A Book on Self-Empowerment

Compiled by
M. M. Walia

NEW DAWN PRESS, INC.
USA • UK • INDIA

NEW DAWN PRESS GROUP

Published by New Dawn Press Group
New Dawn Press, Inc., 244 South Randall Rd # 90, Elgin, IL 60123
e-mail: sales@newdawnpress.com

New Dawn Press, 2 Tintern Close, Slough, Berkshire, SL1-2TB, UK
e-mail: salesuk@newdawnpress.org

New Dawn Press (An Imprint of Sterling Publishers (P) Ltd)
A-59, Okhla Industrial Area, Phase-II, New Delhi-110020, India
e-mail: info@sterlingpublishers.com
www.sterlingpublishers.com

For a better life – Fearlessness

© 2006, Sterling Publishers (P) Ltd
ISBN 1 84557 577 6

All rights are reserved. No part of this publication may be reproduced, stored in a retrieval system or transmitted, in any form or by any means, mechanical, photocopying, recording or otherwise, without prior written permission of the publisher.

PRINTED IN INDIA

Where the Mind is without Fear

Where the mind is without fear
and the head is held high;
Where knowledge is free;
Where the world has not been
broken up into fragments by
narrow domestic walls;
Where words come out
from the depth of truth;
Where tireless striving stretches
its arms towards perfection;

Where the clear stream of reason
has not lost its way into the dreary
desert sand of dead habit;
Where the mind is led forward by Thee
into ever-widening thought and action –
Into that heaven of freedom,
my Father, let my country awake.

— Rabindranath Tagore

The Lord is my shepherd and
I shall not fear.
— The Bible

Fear is a temporary state of mind.
As such it is nothing to be ashamed of.
It is good,
a definite protection given to us

by God to preserve us.
Fear, the urge to escape,
only becomes a bad thing
when it overpowers us.

– Anon

The Power of Fearlessness

❖ Fear is undoubtedly the most delibilitating emotion which affects all human beings, in lesser or greater measure, with the worst form of negative influence on their behaviour. 'Fearlessness' is, thus, the most virtuous trait of the personality not only for the soldier, but for everybody. Courage, and more importantly moral courage, is one of the greatest assets of a successful man. There can be no worse disease than cowardice.

❖ In fear lies the genesis of many other negative elements of human behaviour. Fear of losing what one has and apprehension of not getting what one desires, leads to considerable stress and strain in life. 'Fear of the Unknown' is a common source of anxiety and worry. Fear manifests itself into many a crime too. The worst form of fear is phobia when fear becomes irrational.

- ❖ Achievements resulting from fear are not long lasting and thus not worthwhile. Discipline which has fear as its dictating force is only skin deep. It is thus erroneous to subscribe to the idea that fear does have a positive role too. Even spiritual reverence based on fear of God is totally irrelevant. That is why Sathya Sai Baba says — "Why fear when I am here?"

Fearlessness – The Foremost Virtue

- ❖ Fearlessness (*abhaya*), has been given the first place amongst the twenty-six divine virtues of a man listed in the *Bhagavad Gita*. This is not a mere accident, but deliberate. Without truth, good qualities have no value; but then, for truth, fearlessness is essential.

- ❖ In an atmosphere charged with fear, good qualities cannot grow; in fact, they become bad qualities, and good efforts and tendencies get weakened. Fearlessness is the 'commander' of all good qualities; but the army has to be watched from the front and rear, and on both sides. The direct attack will, of course, be from the front, but it may also be stealthily set upon from behind. While, in front, fearlessness stands alert, humility guards the rear. This is an excellent arrangement.

❖ If we have all the twenty-five of these qualities, but have egoism or pride *(ahamkara)* in these, there is every chance of a stealthy attack from behind in which we shall lose all that we have now. That is why, humility is at the rear of the list. In the absence of humility, there is no knowing when victory will turn into defeat. Thus, by placing fearlessness in front, humility at the rear we can develop all the good qualities.

— *Talks on the* Gita *by Vinoba Bhave*

❖ Fearlessness is not a characteristic feature only of a spiritually-elevated person. It can become a necessary day-to-day attitude of the life of every individual.

❖ Proper estimation and awareness of one's own inherent capacities is the first step towards developing self-confidence, leading to fearlessness.

❖ Life is essentially the present moment with its innumerable opportunities. And, it can only be lived if one overcomes the fears with reference to the past and the future, and if one utilises all that it offers in the present.

— *Swami Nischalananda*

❖ Man is assailed by three kinds of calamities. He is afraid of natural forces, the caprices of society in which he lives, and also of the unknowable will of God. Confronted by these three factors, man spends at least the earlier part of his life in fear. Thereafter, when he turns to light, or wisdom, the sole purpose of his search is to have release from these threefold calamities.

❖ That is why fearlessness is given first place in the enumeration of divine virtues. The instrument for such a search is an unpolluted mind; hence, the reference to the purity of the self after the mention of fearlessness.

— Commentary on the *Bhagavad Gita*
by *Nitya Chaitanya Yati*

Fear is generated in one,
only when one is in a field which is clouded
by ignorance. Fear is the expression of
ignorance (avidya).
Where there is knowledge
there is
fearlessness (abhayam).
– Commentary on the "Holy Gita"
By Swami Chinmayananda.

Absolute Fearlessness

Nervous excitement caused by the apprehension of losing something which is agreeable and meeting with something which is unwelcome is called '*Bhaya*' or fear, eg, the fear of loss of prestige, fear of ignominy, fear of scandal, fear of ailment, fear of punishment by law, fear of ghosts and evil spirits, fear of death, etc. The total absence of all these fears is called '*Abhaya*' or absolute fearlessness.

— '*Srimad Bhagavad Gita*'
Commentary by Jayadayal Goyondaka

The Genesis of Fear

Looking Backwards

The sense of guilt, or a lack of faith, makes fear do something else to a person. It produces a looking backward, a recollection of past mistakes and misfortunes. The result is a vicious circle; looking back brings fear, and fear brings looking back.

Crossing Bridges

There are any number of poor souls who consume all their constructive power in crossing needless bridges. We are constantly occupied over what may happen, but which never does happen in the form we imagined. And if by chance the worst comes, is it ever as bad as we feared?

Guilty Conscience

Fear has its roots in guilt, or in lack of faith, or in vain regrets, or in morbid anxiety about the future. This bad state of the psyche does something to us physically and mentally, as well as spiritually.

Effect of Fear

- Physically, fear can actually kill; it is so powerful in its effect on the body. From the physiological point of view, when fear presents itself to the mind, the whole body reacts, so that all but the most absolutely necessary functions cease. Digestion stops. Blood from the stomach rushes to the arms and legs. The heart beats faster. Blood sugar is secreted rapidly for extra energy. The pupils of the eyes dilate to let in more light for greater vision. Muscles immediately grow tense.

- Since we cannot work off this surplus physical power caused by fear, the body suffers. Thus the person filled with fear is shortening life by hurting the body.

- Mentally, fear creates further havoc, poisoning the attitude in everyone towards life's relationships.

- Spiritually, long sustained fear tends to cut us off from God. We become like radios with the current turned off, or jammed with "static". If, as St. John says, "there is no fear in love," the statement is also true in reverse: there is no love in fear.

— From *Overcoming Our Fears*

May your fear of Heaven be as strong as your fear of man!

— Talmud Breakot

The fear of the Lord is the beginning of wisdom.

— Proverbs

FEAR Thou NOT for I am with Thee.

— The Bible

Good and Bad Fear

The Instinct To Escape

The instinct to run away from danger is a left over of millions of years of the evolution of primitive man. Is it good or bad? If I alone have to escape danger, it helps me and is good. If I have to brave danger for another's sake, it hinders me, and is bad.

Good Fear

The instinct to run is necessary for self-preservation. The same fear today is a God-given blessing, for if we were not afraid of crossing the street, most of us would never live to reach the other side. Any fear which produces in us a healthy caution is a good fear.

Bad Fear

- Fear, which was meant to save us and act as a stimulus, can get the upper hand and become permanent — a ruling passion. We find ourselves victims, with no control over the situation.

- Fear can lay a paralysing hand upon our better impulses and set up a conflict within us. Such a conflict if unresolved always weakens the personality.

- Normally, a person tries to get rid of the conflict. Sometimes he tries to get rid of his bad fears by putting them outside of his mind completely. This is called dissociation.

- Or, if this is not successful, then he tries repression which means that he keeps pushing his fears down into the unconscious where they seem to be hidden. At least, he doesn't feel them too often, but nonetheless they produce much trouble. The result is that many of the fears we thought we had pushed down deep enough to forget, come up again in all sorts of disguises.

   — From *Overcoming Our Fears*

Fear of Failure

The fear of failure often seriously handicaps the young who have not yet proved themselves. It goads them into terror of examinations, and undue shyness with others.

If, on the other hand, the major thought is simply to do one's best, and when examined, to set down just what we know, we are freed from self-conscious fear, and our ability for good work is immensely increased.

— From *Overcoming Our Fears*

Attitudes to Fight Fear

Mental Attitudes

First of all, we must realise that no logic will prevent fear. We may argue and reason all we like, but fear will come just the same. Habits of mind help replace 'fear' with 'faith'.

Do not Fear Fear

If the mind stops looking upon fear as a wicked ogre, and rather looks upon it as a red light in complicated traffic, then it becomes quite calm. Energy is released to heed the warning.

Use Fear to Fight

Fear gives us a pause for breath in order to meet danger. When the going becomes hard, that is the signal to the mind to summon reserve forces, just as we press down on the accelerator of a car as we approach a rise.

Develop a Curiosity about What is Underneath Your Emotion

Never be afraid of discovering the truth. Seek the cause. Once the root is discovered, the emotional tone of your fear is changed. Psychology calls this the objective attitude. Science calls it the scientific approach.

Do not Fight Fear

Fight the things which make you afraid. Fighting a general fear is like trying to learn to swim by sitting on the beach or reading a book about swimming. If you learn always to attack the thing which makes you afraid, half the battle is already won.

Spiritual Attitude

A man who has faith in God always can accomplish far more than one who has not that faith. He trusts God to care for him. As a result of this dependence, all of man's power is released for the achievement of his vision. There is no hampering sense of fear, of insecurity to weigh him down.

"Perfect love casteth out fear," says St John. Love of self feeds fear, love of God destroys it. How can a man fear, when he knows that surrounding him day and night is the love of God, and that nothing can happen to him which He at least does not permit?

— From *Overcoming Our Fears*

Those who believe in the Quran, those who follow the Jewish scriptures, and the Christians – any who believe in God and the Last Day, and work righteously – on them shall be no fear, nor shall they grieve.

– The Quran

If you have Faith and are consecrated to the Divine, there is a very simple way of overcoming fear — it is to say: "Let Your will be done. Nothing can frighten me because it is You who are guiding my life." That acts immediately. Of all the means, this is the most effective; indeed, it is. That is, one must be truly consecrated to the Divine. If one has that, it acts immediately; all fears vanish immediately like a dream.

— The Mother

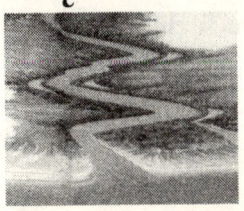

The Philosophy of Fearlessness

Abhayam is the passive freedom from fear with which a bold calmness meets and receives every menace of danger and shock of misfortune.

Fear creates imaginary terrors — even if there is real danger, fear does not help; it clouds the intelligence, takes away presence of mind and prevents one from seeing the right thing to do.

– *Sri Aurobindo*

The Six Ghosts of Fear

There are six basic fears, some combinations of which every human suffers, at one time or another.

- The fear of poverty
- The fear of criticism
- The fear of ill health
- The fear of the loss of someone's love
- The fear of old age
- The fear of death

Fear is nothing more than a state of the mind. One's state of mind is subject to control and direction. So, fear is controllable.

What Fear Does to You

Fear paralyses the faculty of reason, destroys the faculty of the imagination, kills self-reliance, undermines enthusiasm, discourages initiative, leads to uncertainty of purpose, encourages procrastination, wipes out enthusiasm and makes self-control an impossibility.

Fear takes the charm from one's personality, destroys the possibility of accurate thinking, diverts concentration of effort; it masters persistence, turns the will-power into nothingness, destroys ambition, beclouds the memory and invites failure in every conceivable form; it kills love and assassinates the finer emotions of the heart, discourages friendship and invites disaster in a hundred forms, and leads to sleeplessness, misery and unhappiness.

How to Cope With Fear

The six basic fears become translated into a state of worry, through indecision.

❖ Relieve yourself forever from the fear of death, by reaching a decision to accept death as an inescapable event.

❖ Whip the fear of poverty by reaching a decision to get along with whatever wealth you can accumulate without worry.

❖ Put your foot down upon the fear of criticism by reaching a decision not to worry about what other people think, do, or say.

❖ Eliminate the fear of old age by reaching a decision to accept it, not as a handicap, but as a great blessing which carries with it wisdom, self-control, and understanding, not known to youth.

❖ Acquit yourself of the fear of ill-health by the decision to forget symptoms.

❖ Master the fear of loss of love by reaching a decision to get along without love.

Kill the habit of worry, in all its forms, by reaching a decision that nothing is worth the price of worry. With this decision will come poise, peace of mind, and calmness of thought which will bring happiness.

A man whose mind is filled with fear not only destroys his own chances of intelligent action, but he transmits these destructive vibrations to the minds of others he meets.

Even a dog or a horse knows when its master lacks courage and behaves accordingly. Lower down in the line of intelligence in the animal kingdom, one finds this same capacity to pick up the vibrations of fear.

— **Think and Grow Rich**
by Napoleon Hill

Eternal Wisdom

Great importance is given to 'Fear' for the achievement of the ideal in spiritual practice, and the devotee tries to improve himself and becomes worthy of following the spiritual path.

He who has this fear in his mind tries to attain death while living, and through spiritual practice makes an effort to become one with the Supreme Being. He is thus saved from the fear of the forces of the negative power (Angel of Death, etc.).

— *Maharaj Sawan Singh*
(Radha Sami Satsang)

Fear is bad,
Fear of fear is worse,
Fear of failure is worst.
- Anon

Fear that man that fears not.
- Anon

Don't be afraid to take a big step if one is indicated.
You cannot cross a chasm in two small jumps.
- David Lloyd George

From the Adi Granth

They who fear God, fear naught else. They who fear not God, have many other fears. Nanak, this mystery is revealed only when one is ushered into the Court of the Lord.

Without fear (of the Lord) not one hath crossed the ocean of this world. And yea, with this fear is decked the (Lord's) love.

Says Kabir, after careful thought, O Seekers, remember the fact that where there is realisation of the Lord, there is no fear; where there is fear, there is no Lord.

Says Nanak, the soul that adorns itself with the ornaments of fear and love, forever enjoys union with the Beloved.

- Fear always springs from ignorance.

  — *Emerson*

- Where there is no fear, there is no religion.

  — *M. K. Gandhi*

- Let us fear God and we shall cease to fear man.

  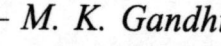
  — *M. K. Gandhi*

- The only thing we have to fear is fear itself.

  — *Franklin D. Roosevelt*

- He who sees all beings in his own self, and his own self in all beings, loses all fear.

  — *Isa Upanishad*

- Who is more foolish, the child afraid of the dark or the man afraid of the light?

  — *Maurice Freehill*

- Fearlessness should never mean want of due respect or regard for the feelings of others.

  — *M. K. Gandhi*

- Fearless minds climb soonest up to crowns.

  — *Shakespeare*

- A man who is afraid will do anything. As fear is a close companion to falsehood, so truth follows fearlessness.

  — *Jawaharlal Nehru*

The moment you fear, you are nobody. It is fear that is the great cause of misery in the world. It is fear that is the greatest of all superstitions. It is fear that is the cause of our woes, and it is fearlessness that brings heaven even in a moment. Therefore 'Arise' awake, and stop not till the goal is reached.

~ Swami Vivekananda

In whatever arena of life he may meet the challenge of courage, whatever may be the sacrifices he faces if he follows his conscience — the loss of his friends, his fortune, his contentment, even the esteem of his fellow men — each man must decide for himself the course he will follow. The stories of past courage can define that ingredient, they can teach, they can offer hope, they can provide inspiration. But they cannot supply courage itself. For this, each man must look into his own soul.

— John F. Kennedy

Eternal Wisdom from Sri Sri Paramahansa Yogananda

Fear can be both constructive and destructive. Loving fear and slavish fear are different. I am speaking of loving fear, which makes one cautious, lest he hurts someone unnecessarily. Slavish fear paralyses the will.

Fear comes from the heart. If ever you feel overcome by dread of some illness or accident, you should inhale and exhale deeply, slowly, and rhythmically several times, relaxing with each exhalation. This helps the circulation to become normal. If your heart is truly quiet, you cannot feel fear at all.

Therefore be cautious, but not fearful. Take the precaution of going on a purifying diet now and then, so that any conditions of illness that may be present in the body will be eliminated. Do your best to remove the causes of illness and then be absolutely unafraid. Whenever you feel afraid, put your hand over your heart next to the skin; rub from left to right, and say, "Father, I am free. Tune out his fear from my heart's-radio." Just as you tune out static on an ordinary radio, so if you continuously rub the heart from left to right, and continuously concentrate on the thought that you want to tune out fear from your heart, it will go, and the joy of God will be perceived.

Fear

Fear is a phenomenon unconsciousness. It is a kind of anguish that comes from ignorance. One does not know the nature of a certain thing, does not know its effect or what will happen, does not know the consequences of one's acts, does not know so many things; and this ignorance brings fear. One fears what one does not know. Take a child, for instance. If it is brought before someone it does not know, its first movement will always be one of fear.

That which is known evokes no fear. That which is perfectly awake, which is fully conscious, also has no fear. It is always something dark that creates fear.

One of the great remedies for conquering fear is to face boldly what one fears. You are put face to face with the danger you fear, and you fear it no longer. From the yogic point of view, the point of view of discipline, this is the cure that is recommended.

When fear comes, if one suceeds in putting upon it consciousness, knowledge, force, light, one can cure it altogether.

If you have faith and are consecrated to the Divine, there is a very simple way — it is to say : "Let your will be done. Nothing can frighten me because it is You who are guiding my life." That acts immediately. Of all the means, this is the most effective.

You must not fear. Most of your troubles come from fear. In fact, ninety per cent of illnesses are the result of the subconscious fear of the body. In the ordinary consciousness of the body there is a more or less hidden anxiety about the consequences of the slightest physical disturbance. It can be translated by these words of doubt about the future: "And what will happen?" It is this anxiety that must be checked. Indeed this anxiety is a lack of confidence in the grace of the Divine, the unmistakable sign that the consecration is not complete and perfect.

— *The Mother*

Fear is hidden consent. When you are afraid of something, it means that you admit its possibility and thus strengthen its hand.

Fear is slavery, work is liberty, courage is victory.

— The Mother

J. Krishnamurti on Fearlessness

What is fear? We are generally afraid of something or of a remembrance of something that has happened. When one is afraid, one has a feeling of danger, a feeling of total isolation called loneliness, deep, abiding, lasting loneliness.

Fear Arising from Insecurity

The mind and the brain need complete security in order to function well — healthily, sanely. Not finding security in anything, in a relationship, in an idea, in a belief — an intelligent mind rejects all that — yet it still looks for complete security. Not finding it, fear comes into being.

Fear and Desire

In coming face to face with fear, we have to understand desire — not the denial of desire but insight into desire. Desire may be the root of fear. The religious monks throughout the world have denied desire, they have resisted desire. They have identified their desire with their gods and with their saviours. But it is still desire. Desire is a form of pleasure. And in the pursuit of pleasure there must be fear also, because, they are two sides of the same coin.

Time – The Root of Fear

What is at the root of fear? Is it time? Time being not just chronological time by the watch but also psychological time, the remembrance of yesterday, pleasure of yesterday and the pains, the grief, the anxieties of yesterday. We are asking whether the root of fear is time. Time to fulfil, time to become, time to achieve, time to realise God. There had been great pleasure yesterday, and one's thought says, "Tomorrow I must have that pleasure again." You have had a great experience — at least you think it was a great experience — and it has become a memory; and you realise it is memory, yet you pursue it tomorrow. So thought is a movement in time, thought as becoming, is the root of fear.

Fear and Meditation

We are not talking of getting rid of fear or suppressing fear; we are asking, can the mind in itself have no cause or substance or reaction which brings fear? Can the mind ever be in a state — can it even have a quality where it has no movement reaching out, where it is completely whole in itself? This implies understanding meditation. Meditation is to be free from fear — both physiological and psychological — otherwise there is no love, there is no compassion. As long as there is fear, no other emotion takes its place. To meditate — not to reach something — is to understand the nature of fear and go beyond it — which is to find a mind that has no remembrance of something which has caused fear so that it is completely whole.

Fearlessness is the first requisite of spirituality. Cowards can never be moral.

Knowing what is right and yet not doing it, is the worst form of cowardice.

Let us fear God and we shall cease to fear man.

— *Mahatma Gandhi*

Fearlessness and the Soldier

❖ Fear is an unpleasant emotion. If intense, it involves presently the whole physiological pattern induced by the action of the sympathetic nervous system. It differs from anger in that it is characterised by an attempt to withdraw from the scene or avoid the fearful situation. The energy, with which the sympathetic system provides the body in a fearful emergency, is normally used for escape, not for attack. Fortunately the energy can, nevertheless, be diverted from flight to attack, and thus fear may come to have a military use.

❖ Fear thrives on frustration. It persists and grows when danger impends, especially if there is nothing the fearful man can do to lessen the threat against him. Action on the other hand, always lessens or may even abolish fear, resolving the frustration and eliminating it.

❖ Fear, as distinguished from anger, is often identical with anxiety, that state of depressed, unpleasant, fatigued, apprehensive worry, which frustration always produces. Fatigue always accompanies prolonged anxiety and also those early stages of fear before the sympathetic system has released enough adrenalin into the blood to abolish it. On the other hand, acute terror, suddenly aroused, is something more than anxiety.

❖ Fear is a normal response to danger and has a use. Unless it takes the form of terror, it energises man for action, yet it also counsels caution, and the most efficient battlecraft has caution as a principal basis. The armed forces can use fear, but they need bravery too, the kind of pride and discipline that makes men fight, because of fear and inspite of fear.

Fighting Fear
Action Dispels Fear

When men are waiting for action, fear is at its height. It generally disappears for most men when action commences.

Knowledge of the Situation Lessens Fear

Fear of the unknown is a a common fear. The unfamiliar is always more fearful than the familiar. Men should therefore be told as much about the enemy and the details of the combat situation to the extent possible.

Habit Makes Fear Less Effective

Fear disorganises, but discipline organises and gets a soldier started on the right action. Then, in action, the mind clears up as fear disappears. Discipline is indeed a soldier's friend in emergency.

Calm Behaviour Lessens Fear

Both fear and bravery are contagious. A successful combat leader is a man who can remain calm in times of crises.

Humour Fights Fear

In trying times and tense moments a laugh can be a lifesaver.

Companionship Decreases Fear

Men, when within sight or hearing of other men in battle, particularly so when in a panic, are reassured.

Religious Faith Diminishes Fear

Men who believe in God's protection and in immortality may be greatly sustained during that period of fear, before a battle. In fact, very few men in battle continue to remain atheists. All reports from the war front show that prayer, as also religious faith, is an efficient enemy of fear.

Loyalty Works Against Fear

Deep loyalty and responsibility to his comrades, to his leader or to his unit as a whole, acts as an antidote to fear. Belief in the cause for which one is fighting is also useful.

Good Physical Condition Works Against Fear

Tired, sleepy, hungry men are much more likely to be fearful than men in good physical condition.

Knowing About Fear Reduces Fear

It is good to remember that fear is a natural psychological emotion common to all. It is good to know that the enemy is also afraid. When a soldier knows that fear in combat is natural, it is highly contagious and almost inevitable, but when the solider knows that courage is also contagious, then part of the battle against fear, is won.

Freedom from Fear

Let the king protect his subjects
from their fear of him,
from their fear of others,
from their fear of each other,
and from their fear of things
that are not human.
— *The Mahabharata*

The Power of the Medal

A mother could not get her son to come home before sunset. So, she told him that the road to their house was haunted by ghosts who came out after dusk.

By the time the boy grew up he was so afraid of ghosts that he refused to run errands at night. So she gave him a medal and taught him that it would protect him.

Bad religion gives him faith in the medal. Good religion gets him to see that ghosts do not exist.

— *Anthony de Mello S.J*

Fearlessness – the Message of The Upanishads

The Upanishads give the message of fearlessness, which has the power to awaken people to the heaven of freedom and delight. Under its influence, people will see the world, and their own life in it, in a new light.

Fear of death, fear of life and fear of being reborn, must give way to an all-round fearlessness. Weakness and cowardice are worse deaths than physical death.

❖ The excessive fear of rebirth among our people received its much-needed corrective not only from Swami Vivekananda's teachings but also from his own personal testament expressed in one of his most passionate utterances:

"And may I be born again and again, and suffer thousands of miseries, so that I may worship the only God that exists, the only God I believe in, the sum total of all souls — and, above all, my God, the wicked, my God, the miserable, my God, the poor of all races, of all species, is the special object of my worship."

Strength – Antidote to Fear

"Strength, O man, strength," say *The Upanishads*, "Stand up and be strong."

❖ How to make man fearless — how to make him cease quaking before the powers of nature, how to make these his servants and not his masters is the one concern of *The Upanishads*. Referring to this redemptive message of *The Upanishads* to all humanity, Swami Vivekananda says —

"And *The Upanishads* are a great mine of strength. Therein lies strength enough to invigorate the whole world; the whole world can be vivified, made strong, energised through them. They will call with trumpet voice upon the weak, the miserable, and the downtrodden of all races, all creeds, and all sects, to stand on their feet and be free. Freedom — physical freedom, mental freedom and spiritual freedom are the watchwords of *The Upanishads*."

❖ Man is subject to all sorts of fears. They subdue him and crush him; he is helpless against them. No worldly knowledge can ultimately save him from fear; when, with its help, he overcomes one fear, ten other fears arise in its place. Only spiritual knowledge can render him absolutely fearless. Ordinary man does not know this — he does not know that in him is a power which is the power of all powers, his own Self, the infinite and immortal *Atman*.

❖ This fearlessness is the fruit of the infinite expansion of consciousness. Then alone will death cease when we are one with existence itself. Then alone will ignorance cease when we are one with knowledge itself. Then alone will sorrows cease when we are one with bliss itself.

— **The Message of the Upanishads**
Swami Ranganathananda

❖ What makes a man stand up and work? Strength is goodness, weakness a sin. There must be no fear, no begging, but demanding — demanding the highest. The true devotees of God are as hard, as adamant and as fearless as lions...Make God listen to you. None of that cringing before God. Remember, God is all-powerful. He can make heroes out of clay. Read what your scriptures say of the Lord,

— calling Him *abhaya* (fearless)! Dare to be fearless, and you will be truly free!

If there is one word that you find coming out like a bomb from *the Upanishads*, bursting like a bombshell upon masses of ignorance, it is the word 'fearlessness'. And the only religion that ought to be taught is the religion of fearlessness. Either in this world or in the world of religion, it is true that fear is the sure cause of degradation and sin. It is fear that brings misery, fear that brings death, fear that breeds evil. And what causes fear? Ignorance of our own nature.

— **His Gospel of Man-making**
Swami Vivekananda

- ❖ The Lord is love. Then why do we fear the Lord? Our adversities are not the wrath of God but our own *karma phala* (fruits of action). We are the makers of our own destinies.

  — *Swami Vivekananda*

- ❖ Be not afraid of anything. You will do marvellous work. The moment you fear, you are nobody.

- ❖ It is fear that is the great cause of misery in the world. It is fear that is the greatest of all superstitions. It is fear that is the cause of our woes, and it is fearlessness that brings heaven even in a moment. Therefore, "Arise, awake, and stop not till the goal is reached."

— Teachings of Swami Vivekananda

> It is not for man to be
> God-fearing;
> But,
> let him be God-loving
> and God-abiding.
> – Swami Parmananda

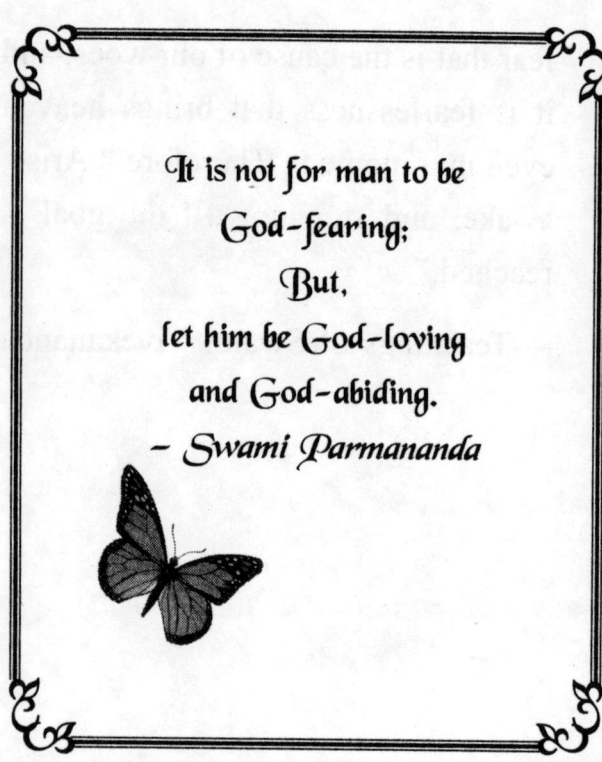